About this book

You may know very little about business apart from everyday events like buying from a shop, seeing lorries carrying goods, eating at a restaurant, and so on. In fact, you cannot live in a modern society without coming into contact with many different sorts of business. This book provides an inside view of the business world.

The book shows how a business can grow from a market stall. It describes all the processes involved in running a successful business, for example researching whether it will work, financing it, selling your product or service, doing accounts, and so on.

Towards the end of the book, you enter the world of big business. There is a look at the Stock Exchange, explaining what it means when a company goes public. You can also find out about business empires and how they are built, and there are some success stories of well known businesses.

Many people who are thinking about setting up businesses are put off by terms such as profit and loss, cash flow, balance sheets, assets and liabilities. On pages 46-47 there is a glossary which gives explanations of these and many other business terms in a clear, straightforward manner.

Pages 16-17 explain how to keep simple financial records for your business. For example, you can find out about useful accounting reminders such as purchase orders, delivery notes and invoices. For more advanced book-keeping advice, turn to pages 40-45. Here you will learn about the books of prime entry, sales and purchase ledgers and the nominal ledger. There is also information on how to check that your books are correct.

Throughout the book you will find a number of puzzles to do with setting up and running a business. They will help you get to grips with some of the trickier accounting tasks. The answers to these puzzles are on page 47.

What is business?

Business is based on common sense. People concentrate on doing certain things that they are good at. They then exchange their work for money, which can in turn be exchanged for the goods or services which they require. This is much more efficient than if each person worked purely to satisfy his or her own needs. There are many different types of business in the modern world. They range from very small ones to enormous multinational companies.

Coal mining and oil extraction.

Trade, service or production?

Every business either provides a service, produces goods, or buys and sells goods and services for a profit (this is called trading). Many are involved in all three activities.

   The picture below shows the main areas of business going on around you every day. See if you can work out which of the three activities each business entails.

The hotel and catering business.

Financial services such as banking and insurance.*

Retail businesses (shops) which sell goods. The word retail comes from the French word *retailler* meaning to cut again. Can you think why? (Answer on page 47.)

BANK

Communications businesses such as telephone, mail and courier services.

Transportation businesses which move materials, products and people from place to place by road, rail, sea and air.

"Small" businesses

About 90 per cent of all businesses are "small"; that is, they employ less than 200 people if they are in manufacturing, or less than ten people for any other business (e.g. retail). About 3,000 small businesses are set up every week in the United Kingdom alone. The next few pages will show you the steps involved in setting up a business of your own.

Public services such as police, fire brigade, armed forces, and local and central governments. These are different from other business activities because in most countries people buy them indirectly by paying taxes.**

*See pages 10-11 and 23.
**See pages 24-25 for more about tax.

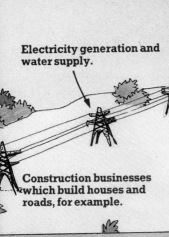

Electricity generation and water supply.

Construction businesses which build houses and roads, for example.

Manufacturing businesses which produce and sell goods, e.g. clothes, cars and food. The word manufacture comes from the Latin *manu factum* meaning made by hand.

Food producing activities such as farming and fishing.

Miscellaneous services including those provided by lawyers, accountants, architects, estate agents, hairdressers and entertainers.

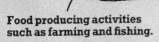

The story of business

In ancient times, business was done by exchanging. A farmer might exchange corn for goats, or sheep for cattle. This is called bartering. But this caused problems when, say, someone had a surplus of goods that no-one needed at that time.

People started to exchange goods and services for tokens that could be stored and exchanged later. The first tokens were shells, sharks' teeth and large stones.

At one time the Romans used cattle as money, hence the word pecuniary which comes from the Latin word *pecus* meaning cattle. See if you can find out the modern meaning of pecuniary.

Later still, gold, silver and copper coins were used. To make them widely accepted, Ancient Greeks put the heads of their gods on the coins and Romans used likenesses of their emperors.

Paper money was first issued in China in about AD650 but was not introduced in Europe until the seventeenth century. It was popular because it was easier to carry than large amounts of heavy coins.

Nowadays, many commercial transactions are done through the banking system without money ever actually changing hands. Financial information is beamed across the world via satellites.

Researching a business

The most important first step for any person thinking about setting up a business is to make sure that they are choosing one which will work. This involves a thorough investigation into the customers' needs. For example, however good you are at car mechanics, your car service will not succeed if very few people in your area actually own cars, or if there is a good local garage which people already use.

On these two pages you can find out the sort of questions you should ask yourself and others in your research.

Choosing a business

It is useful to look at a range of different businesses, rather than picking the first idea that comes into your head. Study existing products and services and see whether you could do better. Then make a list of possible business ventures.

Making jewellery.

Designing and knitting sweaters.

Renovating and selling old bicycles.

Window cleaning.

Now investigate each idea more thoroughly. Philip, for example, is thinking about setting up a window cleaning business. Before going out to buy ladders and cloths, he walks around his neighbourhood knocking on doors and asking questions.

Do you already use a window cleaner? If so, how much do you pay? Are you satisfied with the service? If you don't use one, why not? Do you have modern windows that are easy to clean from inside the house? Would you be willing to pay me to clean your windows? If so, how much?

Being tactful

It is important to ask your questions in the right way, otherwise you may not get truthful answers. For example, people may not want to admit that they cannot afford to have their windows cleaned, so Philip could ask, "How much would you pay to have your windows cleaned?"

Gaining experience

It is a good idea to gain experience before setting up on your own. Offer to provide your service free for family and friends and ask for suggestions on how you could improve. If you are going to supply a product, make things as presents or sell them cheaply to friends. See which are the most popular and offer to make things to order.

Philip is able to get a part-time job with a window cleaner. After a few months he writes a list of the pros and cons of a window cleaning business.

PROS

Not much competition in my area.

Doesn't need much money to start up.

Could also clean people's cars, or do other odd jobs for them once I get to know them. Also, a possibility of diversifying into cleaning factory and shop windows, or office cleaning and other services.

CONS

Physical risks. What would happen if I fell off a ladder and broke a leg? I could be out of action for weeks.

Not much profit in cleaning house windows.

Seasonal fluctuation – fewer people want their windows cleaned in the winter.

Not an essential service, so if incomes drop people could do without.

People are often out when I call, or have no money in the house, so I have to call again for payment.

Weighing it up

After you have studied a few business ideas carefully you will be in a position to decide which is the best proposition. Some need lots of money to start; some need special expertise; with some, location is crucial (retailing, for example). Remember to take all these factors into account in making your choice.

Planning the business

You can now make a detailed plan of your most promising business idea. Ask yourself questions like those on the list below. It does not matter if you are not actually going to set up the business at the moment – it is still fun to plan. Good business people are always assessing their businesses in this way, and adapting them as the market changes.

★ What kinds of customers am I aiming to serve – householders or business people, young or old, rich or not-so-rich?
★ How many potential customers are there in the area I aim to cover?
★ How will I attract customers?
★ What products or services will I offer?

7

Will you make a profit?

Once you have decided on a business scheme which your market research suggests will be successful, you can find out whether you will make a profit. To do this, you need to estimate your costs (how much it will cost you to run the business) and your pricing (how much you can sell your goods or services for).

What are your costs?

Your business costs can be broken down into four different areas: material costs, labour costs, overheads and your own wages. Decide on a time period (say, three months) and work out each of your costs for that period as shown in this picture.

Own wages

This is the minimum amount of money you feel you can live on – remember, unless you have another job you will probably not have any other income coming in.

Material costs

If you are making a product, you will need to buy the materials. Suppose you were thinking of making clothes to sell. First estimate the number of garments you will sell in three months, then work out how much cloth, thread and so on you will need. Remember to include all the tiny items like buttons, as they add up when you make a lot of garments.

Don't forget to allow for waste; mistakes can easily be made in the cutting or sewing.

Calculating the total cost

You can now work out the average cost of each item or, if you are offering a service, the cost of each hour of your work.

1. Add together the costs of your own wages, extra labour and overheads.

2. Divide this total by the number of items you expect to sell, or, if you are supplying a service, the number of hours you expect to be able to charge for.

3. If you are making a product, add this to the estimated costs of material for each item.

What price?

Base your prices on what people have said they would pay for your service, or the price of comparable goods in the shops. Remember if you sell to shops that they will probably add at least 30 per cent for their profit.

If your cost figure is higher than the price you feel you can charge, then you should rethink your business plan. Aim to make at least 10 per cent profit.

8

*You can find out about some of the responsibilities you have towards employees on page 23.
**See pages 10-11.

Labour costs

If you think there will be more demand for your work than you can do yourself, you will need to take on an assistant.* There are many things to take into consideration when estimating how long a job will take such as coffee breaks, giving or receiving instructions, travelling time and dealing with customers. All this can work out at about 15 to 25 per cent on top of the time it takes to perform the task itself.

Estimate how many hours you will need an assistant to put in. You can find out the hourly rate you should be paying from advertisements for similar jobs in newspapers.

Overheads

Overheads are charges incurred in the general running of the business. They include rent, rates, telephone bills, postage, fuel, advertising, insurance, travel, interest on borrowed money** and money spent on the upkeep of equipment. They do not have a direct connection with the actual product which is being made or service being provided. Estimate each bill, and any others you can think of, by talking to other people who have already set up in business.

Sasha's dressmaking

Here is a puzzle to help you see how to cost a business idea.

Sasha estimates that in three months she could sell 150 dresses at $60 each. Using the information on the right, can you work out whether she would make a profit?

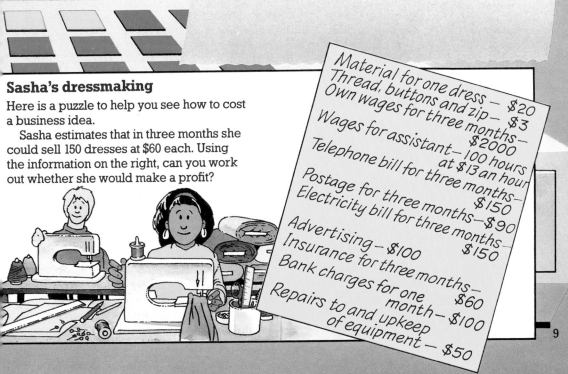

Material for one dress — $20
Thread, buttons and zip — $3
Own wages for three months — $2000
Wages for assistant — 100 hours at $13 an hour
Telephone bill for three months — $150
Postage for three months — $90
Electricity bill for three months — $150
Advertising — $100
Insurance for three months — $60
Bank charges for one month — $100
Repairs to and upkeep of equipment — $50

9

Borrowing money

You will probably be short of money when you set up your business and will need some help in financing it. Below, you can find out how to calculate the amount of money you need to borrow by drawing up a plan called a cash flow chart. There are also suggestions on where you might find a willing lender.

What is cash flow?

Money does two things in a business – it comes in and it goes out, rather like water in a bath. This is called cash flow. If money comes in faster than it goes out, the business is said to be more "liquid", and money is available for expansion or investment. But if money goes out faster than it comes in, the business can dry up.

	JAN	FEB
MONEY IN FROM SALES	50	75
MONEY OUT, INCLUDING YOUR TOTAL DAY-TO-DAY COSTS, AND THE COST OF EQUIPMENT	1050	250
MONEY IN MINUS MONEY OUT	¯1000	¯175
DIFFERENCE BETWEEN MONEY IN AND MONEY OUT SO FAR IN THE PERIOD	¯1000	¯1175

Borrowing from a bank

This involves preparing a campaign to convince the bank manager that your business is a good investment. This is especially important if you are under 18 because legally the bank cannot force you to pay your debts if your business goes bust. Some banks, however, are keen to encourage young people to set up businesses. Below are the sorts of things which will help you.

Cash flow chart. **Samples of your work.** **Expected sales figures.**

The bank manager may also ask you to provide him with security (a promise that you will sell a valuable possession to pay off your debts if things go wrong), or a guarantor (a friend or relative who agrees to repay the loan if you cannot).

There are two different ways in which you may be able to borrow money from a bank.

1. Overdraft*

This enables you to take out more money than you have in your account. The bank manager will give you a limit up to which you can borrow. You pay interest** on the amount you borrow on a daily basis, so you can pay back some of the money when your cash flow improves and stop paying interest on it. However, the bank manager can ask you to repay your overdraft at any moment.

2. Loan

This is safer than an overdraft because you and the manager agree the period over which you will repay the loan at the outset. However, you pay interest on the whole loan even if you do not need all of it.

10

Overdrafts are only available in certain countries.
**Interest is a percentage of the loan which you are charged on top of the money you pay back.*

Cash flow charts

You can predict how much money will be flowing in and out of the business at any given time by drawing up a cash flow chart like the one below. This will show you how much money you will need to borrow, and for how long.

In May, the chart shows that there is the same amount of money coming in as there is going out. After this, there is gradually more money coming in. As the business takes off, it should be possible to pay back the money you have borrowed

Why is there so much money going out in the first month?

Try drawing up a cash flow chart for a business idea of your own.

MAR	APR	MAY	JUNE
125	200	250	280
250	250	250	250
-125	-50	0	30
-1300	-1350	-1350	-1320

Borrowing from friends

You may have relatives or friends who can lend you money. Keep the arrangement businesslike by drawing up a written agreement showing the amount you have borrowed, what interest you will pay, and when you expect to repay the money.

Grants

Many grants are available to encourage and help small businesses. Check to see whether you qualify for one at your local government offices. Grants are a free gift of money which you do not have to pay back.

Still no money?

Even if you find that no-one will lend you money, there are many businesses which need very little cash at all. For example, if you sell by mail order,* you get cash with the order, so the cash flow situation is better. Also, service businesses can cost you little more than your time.

Credit is when you buy the goods with an IOU slip, promising to pay for them at an agreed time.

Some suppliers may be prepared to give you credit for bulk orders of ready-made goods. You can sell them for cash at a higher price; people are often prepared to pay for convenience. This will give you the funds to pay the supplier.

11

See page 14 for more about mail order.

Establishing your business

Before you can start your new business, there are a number of decisions you still have to make. For example, who should you buy your supplies from? What premises will you work from? How much control do you want to keep in the business? This last question depends upon whether you decide to work as a sole trader, a partnership or a limited company.

The information on these two pages will help you make the right decisions for your particular business idea.

Choosing suppliers

All businesses need supplies of some sort; even services need stationery. Go to several suppliers and then compare their terms and the quality of their service before you place an order.

Suppliers may be hesitant about giving credit to a new business, so you must expect to pay cash at first. If you have your own transport, you may find it cheaper to buy from a cash and carry store as you will not have to pay for delivery.

Remember to check deliveries against your orders and invoices. *

Sole trader

EXPLANATION

You alone have responsibility for the business. You also take all the profits, after paying income tax on them.**

ADVANTAGES

1. You do not have to disclose details of your financial affairs except to the tax authorities (and the Customs and Excise if you are registered for Value Added Tax).**
2. You have the final say in any decisions that affect the company.

DISADVANTAGES

You alone are personally responsible for any business debts; if necessary, your personal possessions could be taken to pay them.

Partnership

EXPLANATION

A partnership is a group of between two and twenty people trading as one firm. They share responsibility for debts, decision making, and the profits.

ADVANTAGES

1. Again, you do not have to disclose the partnership's financial affairs to anyone other than the tax authorities.
2. It can be useful when partners have skills in different areas. For example, one person might be creative and another person organized.

DISADVANTAGES

All partners are personally liable for any business debts, even if they are caused by mismanagement by another partner. So it is essential to know your partners well, and trust them.

12

*See page 16 for more about invoices.
**See pages 24-25 for more about taxes.

Creating an office at home

You may be able to run a small business from your own home. You will need a table, a chair, drawers in which to store files, and a telephone. Before deciding, run through this checklist:

★ Does the contract or lease of my house forbid me to run a business from it?
★ Do I need planning permission for a change of use of the premises? Will I have to pay more rates?
★ Do my family mind? Will I disturb them or my neighbours with late deliveries, visits from customers, etc?

Finding premises away from home

Again, you should ask yourself some important questions before deciding on premises:

★ Shall I rent or buy? (It is usually better to rent premises until the business is well established.)

★ Can I make do with cheaper accommodation which is not centrally located?
★ Can I sell my goods from a market stall, which is both cheap to rent and convenient for customers?

Limited company (Ltd.)

EXPLANATION

A company formed by two or more shareholders who put money into the business in return for a share of the profits. They appoint directors who control the company. A limited company must be registered. You can get help from a solicitor to do this, or you can buy one which is already registered but is not trading.

They are called Incorporated Companies (Inc.) in America.

In Australia and South Africa, they are Proprietory Limited Companies (Pty.).

ADVANTAGES

The financial liability of the shareholders is limited. If the business goes bust*, the personal belongings of the shareholders cannot be taken to pay the debts. You each lose only the value of the shares you own.

DISADVANTAGES

1. You may find it difficult to get credit from suppliers or loans from banks unless you give personal guarantees that you will pay your debts to them. This, though, places you in almost the same position as a sole trader or partnership.

2. In addition to sending details of your financial affairs to the taxman, you must send a copy of your annual accounts to the Registrar of Companies. These accounts must be checked by an outside accountant to prove that they present a true picture of the company's finances.

13

*See pages 36-37.

Selling

One of the most exciting parts of building up a business is when you begin to receive orders for your goods or services. The selling process is hard work, but also extremely satisfying. Some of the ways you can sell your goods or services are described below.

Direct selling

This is when you sell a product direct to the public, e.g. in your shop, market stall, or by mail order. Its great advantage is that by listening to comments made by customers, you can judge the market more accurately. It also means that you keep the profit normally taken by a middle man.

However, if you are making the product yourself it is time-consuming to stop working to deal with customers. You may also have to spend money on publicity (see right), especially if your premises are off the beaten track.

Mail order

You could advertise in newspapers or magazines, inviting customers to order goods from you by post. This is called mail order. Customers send in money with their orders. You may need to give a bank reference to the advertising department of the newspaper and they may also ask to see a sample of your work.

Direct mail

Direct mail is another way of selling by post. You send sales leaflets with order forms to potential customers. This can be uneconomical because the response rate is often low and may not be worth the cost of the leaflets and postage.

Working to order

If you provide a service or make personalized goods, you need to encourage orders from customers. Although many may come as a result of recommendations from satisfied customers, you must place yourself firmly in the public eye by promoting yourself.

How to promote yourself

★ Print leaflets, giving information about yourself and your work. You can deliver these to local houses, or ask friends to put them up on school or work noticeboards.

★ Write to magazines and local papers with interesting information about your work. Journalists are often looking for topics for their articles.

Look in the advertising section of newspapers and magazines for ideas on how to design an advertisement. Then try to draw one up for your business.

Selling to shops

If you sell your goods to retailers, you have to spend time calling in to shops with samples as you try to win orders. At first, you may feel that this is taking up too much of your production time and that your work is suffering. However, when you have established some satisfied buyers who place regular orders with you, the time you have to spend on selling will be less.

On the right, there are some tips on how to sell to shops.

★ Advertise in newspapers, specialist magazines, or on the local radio station. Remember to include a telephone number or address where you can be contacted. Budget for repeating your advertisement several times as a single one is rarely effective.

★ Create and keep a professional image. You should give the impression of confidence, and, above all, never be late for an appointment.

Well-designed letterheading is essential, and any packaging should give a feeling of quality.

If possible, make an appointment to see the manager or chief buyer.* Find out the name of the person you are going to see beforehand by asking another member of staff (e.g. the switchboard operator when you telephone).

Prepare what you are going to say and show; remember that shopkeepers are busy people, so be concise. Mention any aspects which might influence the shopkeeper in your favour – quality of materials, quick deliveries, etc.

Listen to the shopkeepers' reservations and see if your product can be adapted to suit their needs. Think about offering discounts for large orders or prompt payment, and help small shops by making eye-catching displays for your goods.

Customer files
Make a card index with the names and addresses of all your customers and potential customers, with comments about their particular needs and preferences. Remember to keep it up to date.

15

*You can find out about the role of a buyer on page 27.

Keeping the books

It is necessary to keep records of the financial affairs of even the smallest business. There are three main reasons for this. Firstly, they will remind you to pay your bills and collect your debts from customers on time. Secondly, you can see how much money you are making (or losing). Finally, they will enable you to work out how much tax you should pay.

You can find out how to keep clear, simple accounts below. For more sophisticated book-keeping methods, see pages 40-45.

Accounting reminders

Here are three papers which will be particularly helpful in reminding you of all your purchases and sales. You can either use standard stationery from a shop, or get some printed on your own headed paper.

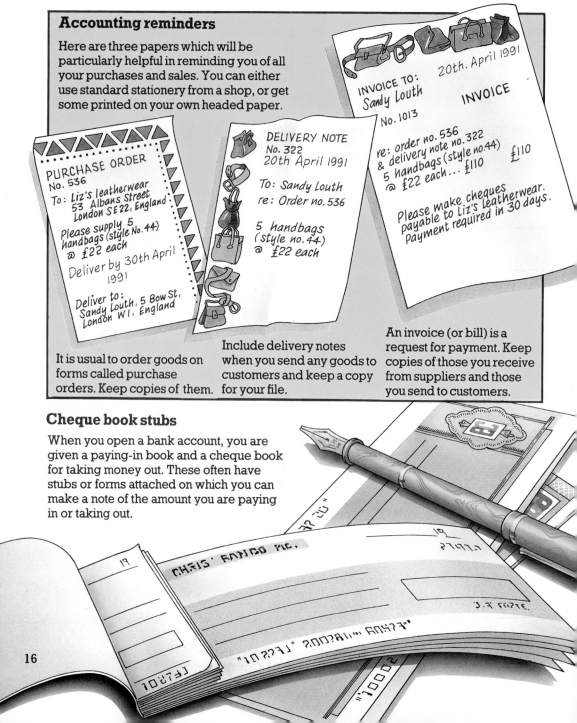

PURCHASE ORDER
No. 536
To: Liz's leatherwear
53 Albans Street
London SE22, England

Please supply 5
handbags (style No.44)
@ £22 each

Deliver by 30th April
1991

Deliver to:
Sandy Louth, 5 Bow St,
London W1, England

DELIVERY NOTE
No. 322
20th April 1991

To: Sandy Louth
re: Order no. 536

5 handbags
(style no. 44)
@ £22 each

20th. April 1991

INVOICE TO:
Sandy Louth

INVOICE

No. 1013

re: order no. 536
& delivery note no.322
5 handbags (style no.44)
@ £22 each ... £110   £110

Please make cheques
payable to Liz's leatherwear.
Payment required in 30 days.

It is usual to order goods on forms called purchase orders. Keep copies of them.

Include delivery notes when you send any goods to customers and keep a copy for your file.

An invoice (or bill) is a request for payment. Keep copies of those you receive from suppliers and those you send to customers.

Cheque book stubs

When you open a bank account, you are given a paying-in book and a cheque book for taking money out. These often have stubs or forms attached on which you can make a note of the amount you are paying in or taking out.

Keeping records

It is useful to keep a record book of money put into the business and money taken out, entering each bill as it is paid. For a very simple system, all you need is a loose leaf binder and two sets of sheets, one for expenditure and one for sales. Every month or so, you should total up the money which has come into the business and what has gone out.

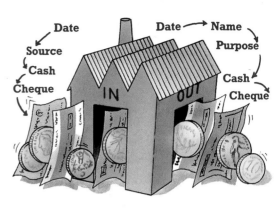

Profit and loss

Using the information from these record sheets, you can draw up a profit and loss chart, like the one on the lorry below.

A profit and loss chart enables you to work out how much profit you have made during a given period. There are two things to take into consideration on top of the amount of sales and expenditure.

1. The cost of unsold goods you had at the start of the period (this is called opening stock), and of those you have at the time of drawing the chart (closing stock).

2. The decreased value of your equipment (this is called depreciation).

What is depreciation?

Say you were running a furniture removal service. For £30,000 you buy a brand new van which you estimate will last you about five years. To spread the cost of this large sum over five years, you could "write off" £6,000 from your accounts each year. This represents the decrease in value, or depreciation, of the van. If you want to replace the van in five years' time, you could open a savings account and put in £6,000 each year from your profits.

Profit and loss from 1st Jan to 31st March
IN
Sales 100
OUT
Expenditure 80
Depreciation 2
Opening stock 8
Less closing stock .... (10)
80
Profit 20

Dupont's restaurant

From the information here, can you draw up a profit and loss chart for Monsieur Dupont?

At the beginning of the month, Monsieur Dupont's opening stock is worth 500 francs.

He spends 1,800 francs on food, wine, overheads and so on. The monthly takings total 3000 francs.

His closing stock is worth 200 francs. This month's contribution towards equipment etc. is 100 francs.

Growing bigger

Your business is doing well and you are thinking about expanding it. But take care; many small businesses make the mistake of growing too fast or in the wrong way. Before you make a firm decision to expand you should be confident that you can find new customers, products, premises, staff, and, most important of all, more money. Some of the problems you may be faced with are described below, and you will also find some suggestions on how to raise more money.

Finding more customers

This may not be easy. For example, if you have a shop, there is a limit to the distance that customers will travel. If you are providing a service, the time and cost of travelling to areas further afield could cut heavily into your profits.

Thinking up new ideas

This involves spending both time and money on researching the market and developing the new products or services to make sure that they meet the customers' requirements (see pages 20-21).

Training extra staff

Depending on your sort of business, you may have to train new staff.

Finding bigger premises

Expanding the premises of a small retail business could mean creating extra floor space by buying the shop next door, for example. Alternatively, you could buy a shop some distance away, but since you cannot be in two places at once, you will need reliable staff.

In a manufacturing business, expansion may mean building an extension to the premises or moving to bigger premises. Bear in mind the disruption to production when moving equipment.

Raising more money

All of the things described above cost money, and you should make sure that you can finance the growth of your business from the start.

Chris, for example, is running a picture framing business. He wants to expand his business by 50 per cent.

He first writes himself a chart called a balance sheet. A balance sheet gives you an instant assessment of where your money is in the business on any particular day – a sort of financial snapshot.

A balance sheet is divided up into assets (what the business owns) and liabilities (what the business owes).

Balance sheet of Wooden Frames Ltd, on 27th May 1991

LIABILITIES

Share capital (money the shareholders and I have put into the company)	4,000
Retained profit (profits reinvested in the company)	3,000
Money owed to suppliers, etc.	1,500
Money owed to bank (overdraft and loan)	1,500
Total liabilities	10,000

ASSETS

Premises	3,000
Equipment and vehicles (valued at their depreciated price, not what was originally paid for them)	2,000
Cost of stock (wood and ready-made frames) not yet sold	3,000
Money owed to the business by customers	2,000
Total assets	10,000

What would the figure for retained profit be if you owed 2,000 to the bank?

18

The advantages of growing bigger

★ It is easier for a big business to get credit from suppliers or to raise loans from banks.
★ It is often cheaper to produce and sell in larger quantities because some costs (such as advertising) may stay the same, but can be spread over more goods. This is called economy of scale.
★ When a big business gets into financial trouble it may be able to turn to the government for help. Governments sometimes offer subsidies or loans to avoid problems such as regional unemployment.

Where can Chris get this money from?

Chris's total assets are 10,000 and his share capital, creditors, and overdraft only total 7,000. A balance sheet always balances, that is, the liabilities equal the assets. So the shareholders have a retained profit of 3,000. This is known as the "balancing figure".

From this chart, Chris can see how much money he will need to expand his business by 50 per cent.

Chris can safely increase the money he owes the bank and his creditors by 50 per cent. This gives him 1,500, but he still needs another 3,500. Below are some suggestions for where he can raise this money.

Money needed to expand by 50 per cent

Extra premises:	1,500
Extra equipment:	1,000
Extra stock:	1,500
Extra debtors:	1,000
	5,000

He could rent the extra premises and hire or lease the extra equipment rather than buying them. Alternatively, he could sell his present premises and rent them back.

He could ask his shareholders to put in the extra money, thus increasing the share capital. But they may not be prepared to, or may not have the money.

He could wait until the business has made that money in extra profit; but this could take several years.

Expanding sales

As your business grows, it is necessary to rethink your sales plan so that you can encourage and cope with increased demand. You can find out some ways of doing this on these two pages.

Mail order

To expand your mail order business, it may be a good idea to identify the sort of customers who buy most of your goods and then try "target mailing". This means sending out sales literature to lots of people who are likely to be interested in a product. It is possible to buy lists of names and addresses of particular groups of people (for example, women aged 35-40 in the middle income bracket) from advertising agencies.

Another way of selling by mail order is to persuade magazines to run a special offer from your range of goods. You sell your product to the magazine at a discount (say 30 per cent) and the magazine then adds a small sum to cover the cost of the page involved, and the cost of sending out the goods. It then offers it to the reader for a sum less than the shop price. You may even be able to persuade the magazine to include your catalogue when sending off each order.

Direct selling

If you have your own retail outlet, such as a market stall or shop, you may decide to grow by increasing the size of the outlet or by buying or renting another outlet. Alternatively, you can rent space in a department store, employing your own sales staff. Many department stores now offer this "shop-within-a-shop" scheme because it allows them to employ fewer staff and have less money tied up in goods.

Selling through agents and sales reps

If you have been selling to shops, or some other retail outlet, you will probably not have time to go round more outlets to sell your goods. You may need to employ sales representatives (reps) or agents.

Agents are people who have a number of contacts and a specialist knowledge in a particular field. They work freelance for several clients at once. They make their money by taking a percentage (say ten per cent) on everything they sell.

It is possible to employ sales reps who work for you alone. The main advantage of this is that you can organize regular sales meetings, say once a month, where they can discuss with you and other members of your staff any suggestions or problems they have come across. They could also provide you with weekly sales reports giving any comments that customers have made about each product.

You have to pay their expenses, and may need to provide them with company cars.

Working to order

To increase the amount of work you do to order, it might be a good idea to try to attract customers with more money to spend. For example, you may have a catering business, where you do cooking for private parties. If you wrote to various companies, explaining the range of cooking you could offer, with some sample menus, you could obtain some really big orders such as regular Board Room lunches.

Price cutting

One way to attract customers from your competitors is to lower your prices. It is important to do your sums carefully to ensure that the increased sales will be enough to cover the lost profit on each item.

In the diagram below, you can see what happens to your costs and profit when you cut your prices. Of course, if your sales go up considerably, your overheads may increase and you may have to take on extra staff.

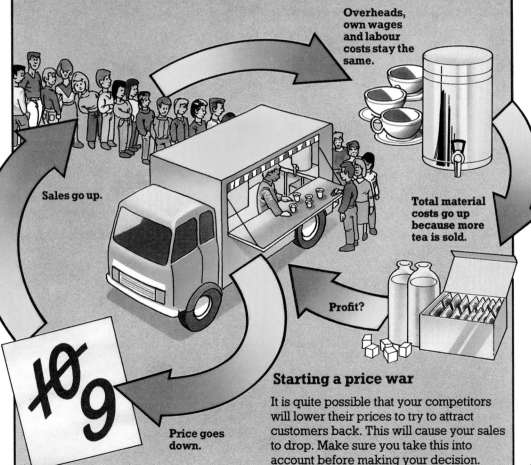

Overheads, own wages and labour costs stay the same.

Sales go up.

Total material costs go up because more tea is sold.

Profit?

Price goes down.

Starting a price war

It is quite possible that your competitors will lower their prices to try to attract customers back. This will cause your sales to drop. Make sure you take this into account before making your decision.

Points of law

On these two pages you can find out about some of the rights of a customer, of a tradesman, and of an employee. These people have differing interests in the world of business and so it is necessary to have laws to ensure that the rights of each are clearly defined. There is also some advice about insurance and the sort of disasters someone in business ought to insure against.

Customers' rights

Customers are entitled to expect goods to be fit for normal use. For example, a chair should withstand the weight of a normal human being.

Retailers must ensure that the goods on sale are free from defects, and must refund the money or offer to replace the goods if they are substandard. They can then take up the matter with their supplier if they wish.

Customers can expect a service to be done well, and can demand that the job is done again if it is done badly the first time. Ultimately, they can ask the culprit to pay for the cost of someone else putting the job right.

It is illegal to describe goods falsely either in advertisements, or verbally. Also, a trader cannot state that goods are reduced unless they have been at a higher price for a minimum period. (In the UK this is 28 days during the previous 12 months.)

Government watchdogs

Officers are employed by governments to check that laws are not being broken. They have the authority to enter shop premises and confiscate goods if necessary.

These officers can also check scales and other measuring devices such as petrol pumps. Traders might try to cheat customers by adjusting their scales to show a heavier weight.

Traders' rights

Traders may not challenge customers suspected of shop-lifting until they have removed the articles from the premises. They can then make a citizen's arrest and call the police who will take action if appropriate.

Any trader may insist that customers provide a banker's card if they wish to pay by cheque, to ensure that it is honoured by the bank.

If customers return goods which they have used, the retailer can refuse to refund the money or exchange the goods.

Employees' rights

In many countries, an employer must supply the employee with a contract of employment. The minimum amount of information you should put in it is listed on the right. These terms cannot then be altered without both parties' agreement. It is also illegal to discriminate against any employee because of colour, race or sex.

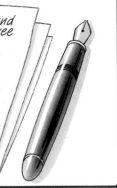

Name of employer and employee
Job-title
Starting date
Rate of pay (payable weekly or monthly)
Hours of work
Holidays and holiday pay
Sick pay
Pension scheme arrangements
Period of notice that should be given if employee wants to leave or employer wants to discharge employee.

Judge for yourself

Can you decide who is probably in the right in the following disputes?

Alan is at the cash till, about to pay for the goods in his trolley. However, the shopkeeper has seen him pocket some other items and challenges him. Can the police prosecute him?

Martin buys some climbing boots. Wearing them on his next climbing trip, he finds them very uncomfortable. Can he demand a refund at the shop he bought them from?

Suzie buys some yoghurt, but finds it is mouldy. The shopkeeper says that since she bought it before the sell-by date on the carton, she must complain to the manufacturer. Do you think this is true?

Insurance

Insurance allows you to take risks with less worry about what would happen if a disaster occurred.

The insurance company estimates the chances of an event happening, for example your premises catching fire. It then charges you a fee (called a premium) based on this estimate. In return, the insurance company guarantees to cover the cost of your loss.

It is possible to insure against almost any event, but the premiums may be so high that it is not worth your while. The picture on the left shows some hazards you might insure against.

Taxation

Many governments collect taxes from both private individuals and businesses to pay for schools, prisons and so on. Businesses have to pay various types of tax, some related to sales, some related to profit, some related to wages, and some related to local government. On these two pages you can find out about these various kinds of taxes.

Value Added Tax

In many countries a tax is added to the price of goods and services. In Britain this is called Value Added Tax (VAT). Businesses which have a high turnover* (in April 1991 this was judged to be £35,000 or more per year) must register for VAT.

This means that you must add the tax on to the price of your goods or services, and pay this to the government about every three months. However, before doing so, you can deduct any VAT you have paid to your suppliers, so make sure you keep a record.

How much VAT does Harry have to add to his bill for painting the room?

Can you work out how much VAT Sue has to pay to the government per tin of paint?

A large manufacturing company produces paints. They charge retailers £10 per can, and add on VAT of 17.5%, making a total price of £11.75.

Harry is a decorator. He charges his customers £10 per hour for his time, plus the cost of the paint, which he buys from Sue. It takes him six hours to decorate one room, and two cans of paint.

Sue runs a home decorating shop. She buys the paint at £11.50 and sells it at £15 + 17.5% VAT = £17.63

Sales tax

In some countries, such as the USA, there is a sales tax instead of VAT. The difference is that sales tax is only put on at the final stage, when the shop sells goods to the general public. Unlike VAT, sales tax is not usually added to services.

It is a much simpler system than VAT, but it does make it easier for people to slip through the system without paying sales tax. Dishonest people may claim that they are going to sell goods which they in fact keep.

*Turnover is the total income from sales during a period.

Income tax

In many countries, people are charged income tax on the money they earn. They pay a percentage of their annual income. Often it is the responsibility of the employer to deduct this from their pay and pass it on to the government. The employer must always keep a record of the amounts earned by each employee and the amount of tax that has been deducted.

Business tax

All businesses have to pay tax on their profits. How much tax you have to pay will be calculated according to your total income from sales minus your business expenses. This is why it is so important to keep accurate records of your expenditure (see pages 16-17).

National insurance

This is another kind of tax which employees in many countries have to pay as well as income tax. It goes partly towards financing state pensions (a payment made to retired people above a certain age) and social security, and partly into general taxation funds.

Building tax

In many countries, people who own premises have to pay a tax on them. The amount they have to pay is assessed according to the building's value, what sort of facilites it has, and so on.

A shop in the high street is liable for a higher tax than the same size shop elsewhere.

If you operate a business from home, you may have to pay more tax than if you were just living there.

How can computers help in business?

Computers can be a great help in the routine tasks of a business. You can buy programs to do the following things:

★ Keep a record of each customer's account, calculating how much each owes and showing overdue bills.
★ Keep a record of VAT charged to customers and paid to suppliers.
★ Give up-to-the-minute balance sheets, cash flow charts, and profit and loss charts.
★ Analyze sales figures to show any significant trends in the market.
★ Print out routine reminders to customers about paying their bills, or mail shots telling them about a new service.

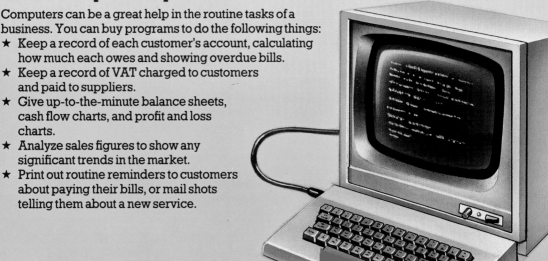

Protecting your ideas

You may have spent a great deal of time and money developing a wonderful new invention, and then the moment you put it on the market, someone copies you and steals half your customers. Two ways of making this illegal are described below and you can also find out about charging people money for copying your ideas.

Copyrighting

Many things can be protected by copyright including computer software, dress designs, books, artwork, and even design drawings and plans for manufactured goods. You can claim copyright by marking your work with the symbol ©, your name, and the year you completed it.

Patenting

You can patent an invention. This forbids anyone else from making and selling anything which uses your idea. However, it is necessary to apply for a patent and it can take up to two years to be processed. So make sure you put in your application well before you plan to sell your product.

Franchising

You can charge people money for selling goods identical to yours by granting them a franchise, or licence, in return for a percentage of their profits.* In this way, you can increase your sales without having to find extra finance.

Alternatively, you may wish to obtain a licence from others. The main advantage of this is that you start with a better knowledge of the costs, probable sales, and profits because you have the benefit of their experience.

The story of McDonald's

In 1937, Ray Kroc started a small business dealing in multimixers: machines which made lots of milkshakes at once. He found that a small restaurant in California, run by Mac and Dick McDonald, bought more multimixers than anyone else.

Despite the popularity of their hamburgers and milkshakes, the brothers did not want to expand. So in 1954 Kroc bought a licence from them to open restaurants like theirs anywhere in the USA in exchange for half a per cent of his sales income.

In 1961 Ray Kroc decided to buy the name McDonald outright for 2.7 million dollars. By the mid 1970s there were McDonald restaurants all over the world.

In 1988, the chain's sales were about 16 billion dollars a year.

*This is normally about 6%.

Stock control

Although it is important that businesses do not run out of vital materials, it is also expensive to hold stock which is not needed. A company should operate with as little as possible. It is therefore necessary to have an efficient stock control system to tell you when you need to order new materials.

1. Two-bin method

You have two containers for each item which you keep in the stores. When the first bin is emptied, you order enough to fill it knowing that the amount in the second bin will keep you going until new supplies arrive. Of course, it is important to calculate the size of bin needed for each item.

2. Written records

This involves keeping records to show when deliveries arrive, how much is used of each item, and what the stock levels are at any given time. You can order just enough to ensure that you never run out. Nowadays this is often done by computers. You can even buy programs which automatically produce a purchase order when stocks fall to a minimum level.

You do have to store certain products. Whisky takes about ten years to mature.

Purchasers and buyers

Large companies often employ people who are responsible for negotiating with suppliers. In manufacturing business they are called purchasers, and in shops they are called buyers, but their job is much the same. They may also be in charge of stock control.

Buyers from large shops can lay down standards which must be met by their manufacturers. This not only applies to finished goods, but also to what goes into them.

Food, for example, must be made from the right quality of ingredients in the proportions specified by the retailer.

Buyers will visit each supplier to make sure that products are being made under hygienic conditions.

Exporting

Once you have exploited the market in your home country as far as possible, you may decide to explore markets further afield. This can be very expensive to begin with, however, and you should be certain that your business will be able to stand the initial investment of both time and money.

On these two pages you can find out about exporting and there is also some advice on things to think about before you decide to take your product to foreign lands.

Researching overseas markets

Each country has different needs and expectations, and so you will have to conduct market research on each one separately. You should visit each country and look carefully into the possibilities it offers. You may find that you have to redesign and adapt your products accordingly.

Here are some factors to consider when choosing a market.

1. The potential of your product there. Will the customer want or need it? For example, your beautiful rainwear will probably be left on the shelf in Saudi Arabia.

2. The cost of exporting your goods, including transport, distribution, import taxes, legal requirements and so on. You can then work out a new minimum price which you should charge for your product and compare it with competitors' to see if it is realistic.

3. The competition. Your product should be significantly better than other products already on the market otherwise you will find it difficult to sell to foreign customers.

Selling your products abroad

There are five main channels of exporting. The one you choose will depend to some extent on your product, and also on how much time you have to spend on exporting.

1. Through overseas buyers

Many overseas firms have buyers based in different countries who are looking for goods to import. You can find out the names and addresses of buyers who are interested in your type of product through government bodies.

2. Through an export house

An export house will secure foreign orders for you. In return for a commission, they will take care of the packing, transportation, insurance and finance necessary to export your goods, and they will organize payment for your goods. However, it does mean that you lose all control over the marketing of your goods.

Drawing up a contract

When drawing up a contract with a customer, you must agree the date of payment, how the money will be paid, and in which currency. In these matters, your bank will be a great help, and it may make tactful enquiries for you about your customers through its international links.

You should also agree on the amount of responsibility each of you will take in delivering the goods. This includes not only transportation, but also the cost of insuring the goods from the moment they leave your building to their arrival at their destination.

Government help

Governments often encourage businesses to export goods as it brings more money into the country. Because of this, there are numerous government organizations available to give advice to exporters. For example, there may be a computerized service which will pinpoint market opportunities for your product and you may be eligible for cheap loans or special grants. You can find out more about these organizations from your local library.

Embassies of the country to which you are planning to export can also be invaluable. They will provide specific information such as names and addresses of outlets and companies in their country that might be interested in your product.

3. Employing overseas agents

You can employ foreign sales agents to get orders for your goods from customers in their own country.

4. Selling directly from home

If you deal directly from your own country, it is important that you keep in close contact with foreign customers to ensure that your product is not overlooked. You should also be aware of any changes in the market. This will take up quite a lot of your time.

5. Selling from an overseas sales base

When you are planning to trade a great deal in a particular country it is often a good idea to establish a sales base there. The staff can then be responsible for the entire marketing of the product.

29

Marketing

As a business grows, it may diversify into different products, or lines. A big business may have such a wide range of products that a whole marketing department is dedicated to monitoring sales and developing new lines. The diagram on the right shows what happens before any new product is put on to the shop shelves.

Where do ideas originate?

Marketing teams get ideas for new products from four main sources:

1. Competitors' lines

This is the "me too" source. If a rival company brings out a particular line which does well, the marketing team will explore the possibility of bringing out a similar line to ensure they have a share of the market.

2. Brainstorming

Colleagues, customers, friends and so on are encouraged to make suggestions. Most of the ideas they come up with are impractical, but sometimes a winner turns up.

3. Gaps in the market

The marketing team will be continually looking out for new opportunities. For example, a craze for a new sport will bring opportunities for sportswear and equipment.

4. Overseas products

A member of the marketing team will be responsible for keeping an eye out for products abroad which might be suitable for the home market.

1 Idea: Luxury diet coleslaw

4

Define the product

The marketing people now instruct artists to work on designs for the packaging of the product. They also inform an advertising agency about the product, letting it know the market they are aiming at, what image they are trying to present, what competition there is and why this product is better, and a rough price for it. This gives the advertisers time to prepare campaigns informing the public about the new product.

5

Is the price realistic?

The research and development team can now come up with samples and rough costs and the marketing people estimate how many they can sell in a five year, three year or one year period. They then calculate a shelf price for the product taking into account their company's profit and the retailer's mark-up. After comparing this with their competitors' prices they can see whether it is realistic.
If no: revise. If yes: carry on.

2 Can it be made?

A special department called the research and development department will find out whether the product can be made.

If the answer is no, revise the proposal.

If the answer is yes, carry on.

3 Does the customer want it?

Members of the marketing department will tell a market research agency about their idea, specifying the sort of person they are aiming at. The market researchers then produce a questionnaire which they ask a selected number of people to answer. From this they can gauge the amount of interest there is in the idea, and what sort of demand there may be for it. They will find out information such as how much customers may be prepared to pay for it, and what sort of packaging they prefer.

If the answer is no, revise (they may be aiming at the wrong sort of people) or scrub.

If the answer is yes, carry on.

6 Does it live up to expectations?

The market research agency presents a group of people in the same category as the first group with samples of the actual product. They may have liked the idea of the product – but do they like the actual thing? Will they still want to buy it?

If no: can the product be modified? If not, scrub the proposal. If it can, go back to Does the customer want it?

If yes: carry on.

7 Proceed to launch

The marketing department then arranges for the production team to make the right number of tubs of coleslaw to fit in with their sales forecast.

The marketing people inform sales reps about the product and the market it is aimed at. They decide on any promotional material they would like to support it in the shops, such as free offers, competitions, and so on.

8 Launch

The sales reps sell the new product to retailers, and the marketing team ensures that it is delivered to them at the right time.

Going public

A business can raise enormous sums of money by selling shares in the company to members of the public. This is called going public. When people buy shares they become part-owners in the company. Potential shareholders must be confident that the value of shares they buy will not go down. This means that most public companies are well established.

After first being issued, the shares are bought and sold on a special market called the Stock Market, or Stock Exchange. Although the price of each share sold on the Stock Market may change every day, this does not normally affect the company.

How does a company go public?

2. The advisers advertise the new shares in the national press and financial magazines, inviting the public to apply for shares by a certain date. On issue day, shares are divided out to applicants. People then start selling them on the Stock Market like any other share.

1. The directors* first go to financial advisers who decide a price for the shares they wish to sell. For a fee, the advisers may agree to buy any unsold shares. This is called underwriting. The Stock Exchange Committee then examines the company thoroughly to check that it is financially sound.

London's International Stock Exchange

There are Stock Exchanges in many major cities including New York, Tokyo, Hong Kong, Melbourne and Paris. One of the biggest and most famous is the International Stock Exchange in London.

Two types of people are involved in the actual deals carried out on the International Stock Exchange:

1. Agency brokers
These are agents through whom members of the public buy and sell shares. They often give their clients advice on whether particular shares are likely to go up or down in value. They charge clients a commission based on the value of each transaction.

2. Market makers
These are like stallholders in a street market, but they deal in shares. Their profit comes from the difference between the buying and selling price of the shares; this is known as the "turn". A market maker alters the price of each share according to the demand for it.

Agency brokers and market makers at work. The red strip gives them up-to-date information on events effecting share prices. Photo courtesy of Warburg Securities.

What do you get if you buy a share?

1 Any increase in the value of the share. If the price goes down, though, you lose. You can sell at any time.

2 Dividends. These are a proportion of the business' profits paid out once or twice a year to the shareholders. However, if the company is doing badly, the directors may decide not to pay out dividends.

3 You can attend and vote at shareholders' meetings where policy decisions are made.

A share certificate

> When the majority of share prices go up, the Stock Market is said to be bullish.

Some people try to make money by predicting what will happen to the price of certain shares, and buying or selling accordingly. This is called speculating. There are three main types of speculator; bulls, bears and stags.

Bulls expect prices to rise and buy with the intention of selling at a higher price later.

Bears expect prices to fall so they sell, hoping to buy shares back later at a lower price.

Stags apply for new issues which they believe will go up in price when traded on the Stock Market. They will then sell and make a quick profit.

Price lists

Agency brokers and market makers use their computers to check the prices at which other market makers are buying and selling their shares. The system that provides this information is known as the Stock Exchange Automated Quotations (SEAQ) screen service.

Often a market maker will quote a price but set a limit on the number of shares he or she will buy or sell at that price. This limit is also shown on the computer.

How do market makers and brokers make a deal?

1. Judy asks an agency broker to sell 500 shares for her.
2. The agency broker consults his SEAQ screen to check the prices quoted for the shares by various market makers.
3. He then telephones the market maker offering the best price. The market maker is duty bound to deal at the price he is quoting on the screen, up to his set limit.
4. Both the market maker and agency broker type the deal into their computers. On settlement day (normally every two weeks) the market maker pays the agency broker for the shares. Having deducted his commission, the agency broker sends the money to Judy.

Building a business empire

Some people are ambitious enough to want to build up a business empire. They are motivated by the great financial rewards, power and influence that it can bring. On these two pages you can find out about these empires and how they are built.

Expanding sideways

The company expands by doing the same activities as before, but on a larger scale. For example, an ice-cream manufacturer would produce more and more, eventually cornering a large share of the market.

Expanding upwards and downwards

This is when the company expands into other stages of production in the same industry. So the ice-cream manufacturer might take over the selling side of it too.

Diversifying

The company expands into completely different fields with which it has had no previous connection. So the ice-cream manufacturer might start producing sausages as well. The great advantage is that this keeps the staff occupied and brings money in during the decrease in demand for ice-cream during the winter.

Take-overs and mergers

One way of expanding a business rapidly is by take-over or merger. A take-over is when a company buys enough shares in another company to make it the major shareholder and therefore to have the largest vote. It can then take over the running of the company.

A merger is when two or more companies are joined together to form a new company. The shareholders of each company exchange their old shares for shares in the new company.

Which company?

When looking for companies to take over or merge with, you should obviously look for those which will particularly benefit your firm in some way, such as those shown below.

1. A major supplier or major sales outlet this will ensure you get favourable treatment.
2. A company with a good share of the same market (this will reduce competition).
3. A company with a good technological advantage.

A company about to take over another is called the predator.

A company about to be taken over is called the target.

The shareholders' position

If there are not enough shares on the Stock Market available for a predator to buy, it will make a formal offer to the shareholders of either cash or some of its own shares. In either case, the offer will be higher than the market price, in order to persuade shareholders to sell.

Because the shareholders are in a powerful position, rumours of take-overs often cause the price of shares to rise. If the target company is against the take-over, there can be a long and bitter battle between the two companies, each trying to win the shareholders' support.

Monopolies

A company can grow so big that it is able to eliminate all its competitors and therefore have the market all to itself. This is called a monopoly. The word monopoly comes from the Greek words *monos* meaning only, and *poleein* meaning to sell.

A company could become a monopoly by lowering its prices for a short period thus putting competitors out of business if they are unable to do the same. Alternatively, it can give suppliers large orders so that they no longer have time to work for anyone else.

Anti-monopoly safeguards

Monopolies have a tremendous amount of power because they are the only producers of certain goods. This means that they are able to charge extortionate prices in the safe knowledge that customers cannot shop elsewhere. For this reason there are laws to protect customers against possible monopolies being formed.

International and multinational companies

Very large companies sell their goods all over the world. They can be either international or multinational.

International companies are firms that operate mostly from one country but export to other countries. For example, Toyota makes most of its cars in Japan but they are sold throughout the Western world.

Multinational companies have their headquarters in one country but have factories and offices elsewhere, which operate in many ways as independent companies. For example, General Motors is based in America but own Vauxhall in Britain, Opel in Germany and Holden in Australia. Important decisions are made in America, but the European managers make most of the decisions concerning their own companies without referring to the American headquarters.

Going bust

Not all businesses become empires overnight. Some get into severe financial difficulties and cannot meet their debts. This is known as being insolvent. Below there is advice on noticing danger signals. You can also find out what happens when a sole trader or partnership goes bankrupt, or a company goes into liquidation.

Why do businesses go bust?

The main reason for the failure of most businesses is lack of control of cash flow. When you sell goods or services on credit you should make a profit, but if the customer takes a long time to pay, you could run out of money with which to pay your suppliers and employees.

How to control your cash flow

Just as locks control the flow of water in a canal, you can control your cash flow by taking a number of precautions.

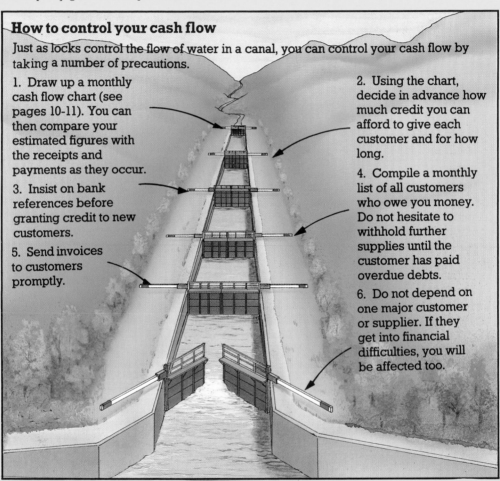

1. Draw up a monthly cash flow chart (see pages 10-11). You can then compare your estimated figures with the receipts and payments as they occur.

2. Using the chart, decide in advance how much credit you can afford to give each customer and for how long.

3. Insist on bank references before granting credit to new customers.

4. Compile a monthly list of all customers who owe you money. Do not hesitate to withhold further supplies until the customer has paid overdue debts.

5. Send invoices to customers promptly.

6. Do not depend on one major customer or supplier. If they get into financial difficulties, you will be affected too.

The bankruptcy procedure

If a sole trader or partnership cannot pay its debts, one or more of its major creditors can ask the courts for a bankruptcy order. The courts will then appoint a trustee who will take possession of the debtor's property. The trustee will ensure a fair distribution of the debtor's property to creditors; this may include stock, assets, equipment and personal possessions.

Having been declared bankrupt, you may not set up a business again unless you have been discharged by the courts. When you are discharged you are free to make a fresh start and your slate is wiped clean. The courts may discharge you after a set period of time, say five years, if you have managed to pay off a percentage of your debts in that time.

Record breaking bankruptcy

One of the biggest bankruptcy cases is that of William Stern. His company, the Willstar Group Holding Company, dealt in buying, developing and selling property. However, in the 1970s, the price of property fell, and Stern's company fell with it. In February 1983, his debts totalled £142,978,413. The courts agreed that he could be discharged in two and a half years' time if he paid £500,000 of his debts.

Liquidation

If a limited or public company builds up large debts it cannot pay, it goes into liquidation. This can either be voluntary or compulsory liquidation. If it is voluntary liquidation, the directors promise to pay all its debts within a certain period (12 months in the UK). However, if the company has not gone into voluntary liquidation, an unpaid creditor may apply to the courts for compulsory liquidation of the company. A liquidator, or receiver, is then appointed to look after the affairs of the company, paying its debts and sometimes winding it up.

In both cases, the directors must prepare a full statement of the company's affairs, listing its assets and liabilities, and why it is in debt. The company must also stop trading.

Directors of large companies sometimes give press conferences to explain the situation to the shareholders.

Priority on debts

If a business is liquidated, some people have a greater right than others to any money or assets belonging to the company. The order of priority is shown below.

Legal fees and liquidator's payment.

Preferential creditors. These include tax collectors and employees.

Secured creditors. These include banks.

Ordinary creditors. These may get very little or nothing.

Shareholders who, depending on the extent of the debts, may lose all the money they have invested in the company.

What to do if your business is going badly

If you have a temporary cash flow problem, there are a number of paths you may be able to follow without going bankrupt or into liquidation.

1. Raise some money from the bank. If the company that owes you money is secure, for example a large, prosperous company, a bank may be prepared to tide you over with a short-term loan.

2. Sell some assets, for example stock, or sell your premises and rent them back.

3. You may be able to sell the business at a low price.

Success stories

Vidal Sassoon

Vidal Sassoon was born in a very poor area in the East End of London. At the age of 14 he got a job at a hairdressers' in the East End of London. He learned the trade by washing and cutting the hair of local tramps; he paid them for the privilege.

Vidal progressed to becoming the manager of a hairdressing shop. Then, in 1959 he created a revolutionary hairstyle which rejected the fashion of back-combing and teasing women's hair. Named "The Shape", it was the first of many fascinating geometrical designs which made Vidal Sassoon famous worldwide.

From designing radical new haircuts, Vidal progressed in three different directions. Firstly, he promoted general health and good looks and co-wrote the best-seller "Year of Beauty and Health".

Secondly, he introduced a complete line of hair care products under the Vidal Sassoon name. By 1977, these were being exported to markets all over the world.

Thirdly, Vidal Sassoon set up numerous hairdressing schools, including the London Academy which has trained well over a million students.

Marks and Spencer

Michael Marks, a Lithuanian Jew, emigrated to England in about 1883 and arrived with no money, knowing no English, and unable to read or write. He set up in business in Leeds as a pedlar of buttons, pins, needles and so on, carrying goods from house to house on his back.

In 1884 he took a stall in Leeds market. Over the stall he hung a board saying "Don't ask the price, it's a penny", a slogan which proved to be very successful.

Michael then expanded by opening more stalls in nearby areas, and in 1891 he established a warehouse. He decided to take on an acquaintance, Tom Spencer, as a partner. They each had shares in the business worth £300.

In 1903 they registered Marks and Spencer as a limited company with themselves as the main shareholders. The company flourished. Soon there were over 50 branches selling a variety of goods.

Some were clothes shops, and this became the pattern for future expansion. However, in 1905 Tom died and in 1907 Michael also died leaving Tom's son, his executor (William Chapman), and his own son, Simon, in charge.

MARKS &

BAZAAR

AD

Laura Ashley

In 1953 Bernard and Laura Ashley started a business printing tablemats and scarves. They used silk screens on an old kitchen table in their small attic apartment in Pimlico, London. They sold their products to small shops and department stores in London. Cash flow was a problem as at the start they had only £10 to put into the business.

Overcrowding forced the production part of the business into a nearby basement where Bernard developed a larger, more efficient printing machine. They produced greater quantities and added furnishing and dress fabrics to their list.

The cost of property made further expansion in London impossible, so they moved to Surrey where they used an old coach shed as their factory. Bernard built an even larger printing machine, and the extra production enabled them to start exporting to foreign markets including France, Holland, the U.S. and Australia.

Increasing orders meant they had to expand the factory. Planning regulations forced them out of Surrey and into Wales where they were able to finance a new factory relatively cheaply. Inspired by the beautiful Welsh countryside, Laura designed two dresses which could be produced at a very low price.

Sales of the dresses were high, but the business could not cope with the credit which their customers expected. Laura and Bernard decided to go direct to the public by opening a shop in London. At first this was not a success. Then Bernard had the idea of advertising the £6 dresses on the underground, giving the shop as a stockist.

Customers poured in and their payments restored the cash flow problem. Profits were ploughed back into more factories, shops and research. Factories were opened in Holland, Ireland and America, with new warehouses in London, Paris and New Jersey. Today there are hundreds of shops all over the world.

In 1917 Chapman and Spencer retired from the board of directors due to a difference of opinion. Marks brought in his brother-in-law, Israel Sieff, to help him.

The company went from strength to strength and they became a public company in 1926. The Spencer family sold some of their shares which by then were worth over 500 times the original £300.

In the later 1940s, the company started a policy of only selling goods bearing their own label, that of St Michael. They improved links with suppliers so that they could control quality, and St Michael goods built up a solid reputation. Seeing that there would be a limit to their expansion in clothing, they diversified into food and homeware items which proved to be just as successful.

In addition to their reputation for quality and value for money, they also built up a reputation for staff welfare. They installed canteens and were amongst the first companies to offer medical and dental services to employees.

Advanced book-keeping

Any business, large or small, must have a record of its financial affairs. The previous section on keeping the books has already shown how to keep simple records. The following pages will look at more complex book-keeping by studying the books of a business called Top Chocs, a small company manufacturing expensive, hand-made chocolates.

Kate, the owner of Top Chocs, buys ingredients, such as sugar and cocoa, and kitchen equipment. She also has a van to deliver her product to shops and restaurants.

It is vital that Kate keeps a careful track of all the money going out of the business and how much money is coming in.

The books of prime entry

Four very important books in the Top Chocs accounting system are shown here. They are called the books of prime entry and are the first books that financial details are entered in.

The cash book

The cash book records all the money going into and out of Top Chocs' bank account. The figures and information for writing up the cash book come from the business's paying-in book and cheque book.

On the left, the cash book records income - money coming into the account from Top Chocs' customers.

On the right, the book records expenses - money going out of the account on Top Chocs' purchases, such as the garage bill for fixing Kate's van.

Each item of expense is also entered into a column which records its type, for example rent or petty cash. These are called "analysis columns".

A page from the cash book (Page 1)

Figures on this line are the totals carried over (brought forward) from the previous page.

The cash paid by The Candy Store that Sylvia paid into the bank on 4 January.

A reference code. "N" stands for Nice Chox; "1" means this entry appears on page 1 of the sales ledger.

The sum total of the three cheques paid into Top Chocs' bank account on 4 January.

INCOME					
Date	Details	Ref.	Sales ledger	Other income	Bank
1 Jan	Balance	b/f		1000·00	1000·00
4 Jan	Candy Store	C2	58 · 75		
	Nice Chox	N1	130 · 00		
	Choc. Factory	Ch2	84 ·00		272·75
9 Jan	Choc. Factory	Ch2	60 ·00		
	Candy Store	C2	89·00		149·00

The sales day book

It is important that the Top Chocs accounts have an up-to-date record of sales and a record of the date customers are sent their invoices. This information is kept in the sales day book. Each invoice is entered into the book on the day it is sent out. VAT, or sales tax, is also recorded.

Calculating the turnover

To work out Top Chocs' turnover from 15 December to close of business on 16 December, Kate adds up the net sales column. What was the result?
(Answer page 47)

A page from the sales day book

Page 4					
Date	Customers' invoices	Ref.	Total	VAT 17.5%	Net Sales
15 Dec	Choc. Factory	Ch 2	84·00	12·51	71·49
	Candy Store	C 2	58·75	8·75	50·00
16 Dec	Candy Store	C 2	89·00	13·26	75·74
	Brown Betty	B 2	117·50	17·50	100·00
19 Dec	Smarts	SM 3	58·75	8·75	50·00
	Choc. Factory	Ch 2	60·00	8·94	51·06

Checking the bank balance

Kate adds up the first column in the cash book headed "bank" (income), and then adds up the second column headed "bank" (expenses). By subtracting the second total from the first, she can tell how much is in the account. What was the total?

The figure that Kate arrives at is called the "balance" - that is the difference between the debits and credits.
(Answer page 47)

Each cheque Sylvia pays to creditors is recorded.

In the USA this is sales tax at 7%.

A column for all other items.

EXPENSES

Date	Details	Chq no.	Bank	VAT 17.5%	Purchase ledger	Rent	Motor expenses	Petty cash	Misc.
2 Jan	R. Frank rent	001	200·00			200·00			
4 Jan	W. Davis mixer	002	46·00		46·00				
	T. Jones cocoa	003	117·50		117·50				
	Cash	004	22·00					22·00	
8 Jan	Dave's Garage	005	82·64	12·31			70·33		
9 Jan	T. Jones sugar	006	80·00		80·00				

The purchase day book

It is just as important that Top Chocs keeps a record of money that it owes to creditors, like the 117.50 to T. Jones for cocoa or the 46.00 to W. Davis for a mixer. All creditors' invoices are recorded in the purchase day book. They should be recorded in the book on the day they arrive at Top Chocs.

A page from the purchase day book

Page 3								
Date	Creditors' invoices	Ref.	Total	VAT 17.5%	Purch-ases	Printing & stationery	Motor expenses	Equip-ment
18 Dec	W. Davis	B1	46.00	6.85				39.15
20 Dec	T. Jones	J2	117.50	17.50	100.00			
22 Dec	Print & Son	P5	48.32	7.20		41.12		
	Van Leasing	VL2	93.00	13.85			79.15	
	White & Co	W2	23.69	3.53	20.16			

The cost of running Top Chocs

Kate wants to know how much it cost her to run Top Chocs from 18-22 December. To do this, she adds up each analysis column in the purchase day book and then makes a grand total of them all.

What was the result?

There will of course be other small expenses recorded in the petty cash book explained below. But the answer here will account for the major expenses. (Answer page 47)

Petty cash book

The fourth book of prime entry is the petty cash book. This book records only minor expenses, like biscuits, coffee and stamps. These items are too small to be paid for by cheque, and money for them is taken from Top Chocs' petty cash fund. This fund is kept in a cash box in the accounts office. When the fund gets low, Kate draws more cash out of the bank to top it up.

The left part of the petty cash book (income) gives details of money coming into the petty cash fund - a stamp sold to a member of staff and 22.00 that Kate took out of the business's bank account to top up the petty cash fund. The right part records expenses, such as 1.99 for envelopes.

A page from the petty cash book (Page 4)

INCOME				
Date	Details	Cash from bank	Other	Total
1 Jan	Balance b/f		4.32	4.32
4 Jan	Cash from bank	22.00		22.00
7 Jan	Sale of stamp		.19	.19

The sales and purchase ledgers

In order to keep a check on individual customers and creditors, Kate produces sales and purchase ledgers. The sales ledger tells her if one of her customers is late in paying an invoice. The purchase ledger lets her know if she is late in paying one of her creditor's invoices. Information for these ledgers comes from the sales day book, the purchase day book and the cash book. Ledgers are not books of prime entry because they are not the first books that details are written in.

The sales ledger

Each customer has his or her own section in the sales ledger. On the left-hand side, Kate enters information about the invoices she has sent out. She does this every day and gets this information from the sales day book. On the right hand side she records information from the cash book when the invoices have been paid.

The balance of the two "amount" columns is how much The Candy Store owes Tops Chocs. (Answer page 47)

A page from the sales ledger

The Candy Store C2

Sales				Income			
Date	Details	Ref.	Amount	Date	Details	Ref.	Amount
1 Jan	Bal.	b/f	147·75	4 Jan	Cash	CB 1	58·75
4 Jan	Sales	SDB 5	92·00	9 Jan	Cash	CB 1	89·00
9 Jan	Sales	SDB 5	42·40				

The purchase ledger

A purchase ledger is operated in exactly the same way as the sales ledger. It covers each account that Top Chocs receives invoices from, like the garage or cash and carry.

EXPENSES

Date	Details	Total	VAT 17.5%	Refreshments	Post & stationery	Misc.
2 Jan	Milk	·34		·34		
	Drawing pins	·72	·11		·61	
3 Jan	Coffee	1·62		1·62		
	Stamps	4·40			4·40	
	Window cleaner	1·50				1·50
7 Jan	Milk	·34		·34		
	Envelopes	1·99	·30		1·69	
10 Jan	Window cleaner	1·50				1·50

Checking the petty cash box

On 10 January, when Kate wanted to check how much money should have been in the petty cash box, she added up the total of expenses and then subtracted it from the total of income. How much money should have been in the box? (Answer page 47) 43

Bank reconciliation

Because there is normally a delay between when a cheque is written and when it is paid into the bank, the balances shown in the cash book and the bank statement may not tally. So every week Kate takes a number of steps to make sure that they do. This is called a bank reconciliation.

How to do it

The first step to reconcile the cash book and the statement is to check and see which items appear in both the cash book and the statement.

Next, items that appear in one and not the other, must be listed. For example, the 149.00 recorded in the cash book as being paid into the bank on 9 January, does not appear on the statement.

Customers' cheques that have been paid into the bank, but do not appear on the statement, are added to the statement's balance.

Cheques that Kate has sent out to creditors, but do not appear on the statement, are deducted from the statement's balance.

If the reconciliation has been calculated correctly then the figure will agree with the amount Kate worked out was in her bank account on 9 January.

The bank statement up to 9 January

Top Chocs				National Bank
Date	Details	Payments out	Payments in	Balance
1 Jan	Balance b/f			1000.00
3 Jan	Cheque no. 001	200.00		800.00
4 Jan	Paid in		272.75	1072.75
	Cheque no. 002	46.00		1026.75
	Cheque no. 004	22.00		1004.75
9 Jan	Balance c/f			1004.75

How to work out the reconciliation

Balance of bank statement		1004.75
Add: Cheques from customers paid into the bank, but not on the statement		149.00
Less: Cheques sent to creditors, but not on the statement	003 117.50	
	005 82.64	
	006 80.00	280.14
Balance of cash book		873.61

At the end of the month

At the end of each month, Kate checks the Top Chocs' books of prime entry for accuracy. She also her monthly balances into the nominal ledger.

Are the books correct?

Kate adds up all the columns in the books of prime entry. The grand total of all the individual analysis columns should equal the total of the "bank" or "total" columns. This is called cross casting and proves that the books have been filled in properly and are completely correct.

The balances of the cash book and petty cash book are then carried forward to the beginning of the next month.

Sometimes the totals do not agree with each other. This either means that they have been added up incorrectly or one of the entries is wrong. When this happens Kate has to check all her figures thoroughly until she finds the error.

The nominal ledger

Every month the balance of each account is written up in the nominal ledger. All this information comes from the sales and purchase ledgers and the cash book and petty cash book.

Below is a page from the nominal ledger which records the monthly balances for Kate's printing, postage and stationery account. On this page most of the figures recorded are money she paid for items, such as envelopes. She also received money as well, when she sold a stamp to a member of her staff.

A page from the nominal ledger

Page 10				Printing, postage and stationery			
Expenses				Income			
Date	Details	Ref.	Amount	Date	Details	Ref.	Amount
22 Dec	Printing	PDB 3	48·31	3 Jan	Sale of stamp	PCB 4	·19
10 Jan	Post and Stationery	PCB 4	7·11				

At the end of the financial year

At this time, Kate prepares her annual accounts from the nominal ledger. She totals the "income" amount column and totals the "expenses" amount column for each account. Then she subtracts the "expenses" total from the "income" total to arrive at a balance.

These yearly balances will show how much money was spent on purchases and other items, and how much Top Chocs earned from its customers.

The tax authorities will need a set of these accounts to check how much tax Top Chocs owes for the year.

Glossary

Accountant. A qualified person who specializes in bookkeeping, auditing annual accounts and financial advice.

Agency brokers. People through whom you can buy and sell shares.

Asset. Anything of value owned by a company or individual e.g. equipment or stock. Also intangible things such as patents.

Balance sheet. A statement of the assets and liabilities of a company at a particular time.

Bankrupt. The state of a person who has more debts than he can pay and therefore is judged by a court to be insolvent.

Bartering. Doing business by exchanging.

Agency brokers. People through whom you can buy and sell shares.

Budget. A financial plan.

Cash flow. The flow of money into and out of a business.

Closing stock. The amount of unsold goods you have at the end of an accounting period.

Company. An organization created for a specific purpose, which has a separate legal identity from the people who combine to form it.

Credit. An allowance of time to repay a debt.

Creditor. A person or company to whom money is owed.

Current assets. Cash and other assets such as stock which are sold in the normal course of trading.

Current liabilities. Debts which fall due in a relatively short period.

Debt. An amount owed.

Debtor. A person or company that owes money.

Delivery note. A note attached to goods when they are delivered specifying what they are.

Depreciation. The decrease in value of equipment due to use or lapse of time.

Direct mail. A method of selling goods or services direct from supplier to customer by sending sales literature through the post.

Direct selling. Selling direct to the public.

Director. A member of a board of directors who make the policy decisions for a company.

Discount. A deduction from the normal selling price, usually worked out as a percentage of the normal price.

Dividend. A proportion of a company's profits which is paid to the shareholders.

Exporting. Selling goods abroad.

Grant. A gift of money given for a specific purpose.

Guarantor. Someone who guarantees to pay a person's debts if that person cannot.

Interest. The money paid by a borrower for the use of the lender's money.

International company. A company which operates mainly from one country but exports elsewhere.

Invoice. A bill.

Liabilities. Money a business owes, both externally (e.g. creditors, overdraft) and internally (e.g. shareholders' capital).

Limited company. A company where the shareholders' liability is limited to the amount they have paid for the shares.

Liquidation. A legal process whereby the life of a company is brought to an end.

Mail order. Advertising goods and selling them by post. (See also Direct mail.)

Manufacturing. The process of making goods.

Market makers. People who deal in shares. goods or services.

Merger. The joining of two or more companies to form a new company. (See also Take-over).

Monopoly. The only company dealing in certain goods or services.

Multinational company. A company with factories and offices in many different countries.

Official receiver. An official appointed by a court to look after the affairs of a bankrupt person or to supervise the compulsory winding up of a company.

Opening stock. The amount of unsold stock at the beginning of a financial period.

Overdraft. A bank loan in which the customer's current account is allowed to go into debt to an agreed limit. Interest is calculated on a daily basis.

Overhead. A cost incurred in the normal running of a business which is not directly concerned with the product or service.

Partnership. A group of people trading as one company.

Predator. A company about to take over another.

Profit. The difference between the cost of providing goods or services, and a higher price at which you sell them.

Profit and loss account. A financial statement showing a business' profit or loss over a given period.

Public company. A company whose shares can be offered to the general public and traded on a Stock Exchange.

Purchase order. A form used for ordering goods.

Rates. An annual tax on the value of a property.

Retailer. Shopkeeper.

Retained profit. Profit which is kept in a business.

Sales tax. A tax charged in some countries on the shop price of certain goods.

Security. A valuable possession which you promise to sell in order to pay debts which you would otherwise be unable to pay.

Share capital. The amount of money invested in a company by its shareholders.

Shareholder. The owner of a share or shares in a company, entitling the shareholder to vote at company meetings and to a share in the profits.

Sole trader. A person with sole responsibility for a company's affairs.

Stock. The quantity of materials and finished goods held by a business.

Stock control. Procedures for trying to maintain optimum levels of stock.

Stock Exchange. Also called Stock Market. Place where shares can be bought and sold.

Take-over. Gaining control of a company by buying a majority of its shares.

Target. A company about to be taken over.

Target mailing. Selling by direct mail by sending sales literature to a specific group of people.

Tax. A sum of money collected by governments from businesses and private individuals to pay for public services.

Trading. Buying and selling goods and services for a profit.

Turnover. The total sales income of a business in a given period.

Value Added Tax (VAT). A tax charged in certain countries (including the UK) on the purchase price of goods and services.

Answers

Page 4
A retailer buys goods (e.g. meat, cheese, cereal) in large quantities, cuts them up and sells them in smaller quantities.

Page 9
Sasha's dressmaking
The labour costs, own wages and overheads total $4,200; that is, $28 per dress. Material costs for each dress come to $23. So the total cost of each dress is $51 Sasha would therefore make a profit of $9.

Page 11
The large amount of money going out in the first month is the sum spent on equipment and so on.

Page 17
Profit and loss chart for Monsieur Dupont
IN
Sales 3000
OUT
Expenditure.. 1800
Depreciation.. 100
Opening stock...500
Less closing stock .... (200)
Profit..800

Page 18
The retained profit would be 2,500.

Page 23
Judge for yourself
1. No; Alan has not yet left the shop.
2. Because Martin has worn them, the shoes cannot be sold to anyone else. Since the complaint is not to do with the quality of the goods, he cannot demand a refund.
3. The shopkeeper is wrong. He should exchange the goods or refund the money, and then take up the matter with the manufacturer himself.

Page 41
The turnover for 15-16 December was 398.29.
Kates balance was 873.61

Page 42
It cost 279.58 to run Top Chocs from the 18-22 December.

Page 43
The Candy Store owes Top Chocs 134.40.

There should have been 14.10 in the petty cash box.

47

Index